At David C Cook, we equip the local church around
the corner and around the globe to make disciples.
Come see how we are working together—go to
www.davidccook.com. Thank you!

transforming lives together

I'D LIKE YOU MORE IF YOU WERE MORE LIKE ME

MEMBER CONNECT GUIDE

I'D LIKE YOU MORE IF YOU WERE MORE LIKE ME

GETTING REAL ABOUT GETTING CLOSE

MEMBER CONNECT GUIDE

JOHN ORTBERG

WITH LAURA DERICO

David C Cook

transforming lives together

I'D LIKE YOU MORE IF YOU WERE MORE LIKE ME
MEMBER CONNECT GUIDE
Published by David C Cook
4050 Lee Vance Drive
Colorado Springs, CO 80918 U.S.A.

David C Cook U.K., Kingsway Communications
Eastbourne, East Sussex BN23 6NT, England

The graphic circle C logo is a registered trademark of David C Cook.

All Scripture quotations are taken from the Holy Bible, NEW INTERNATIONAL
VERSION®, NIV®. Copyright © 1973, 2011 by Biblica, Inc. Used by permission.
All rights reserved worldwide. NEW INTERNATIONAL VERSION and
NIV are registered trademarks of Biblica, Inc.® Use of either trademark for the
offering of goods or services requires the prior written consent of Biblica, Inc.

ISBN 978-1-4347-1191-5
eISBN 978-1-4347-1258-5

Material in this resource is adapted from:
I'd Like You More if You Were More like Me: Getting Real about Getting Close.
Copyright © 2017 by John Ortberg.
Published by Tyndale Momentum, Carol Stream, Illinois 60188. Used by permission.

Related titles:
I'd Like You More if You Were More like Me Leader Connect Guide
I'd Like You More if You Were More like Me DVD
I'd Like You More if You Were More like Me Small Group Connection Kit
I'd Like You More if You Were More like Me Church Connection Kit

All epigraphs and feature quotes within this book, unless otherwise
noted, are excerpted from *I'd Like You More if You Were More like
Me: Getting Real about Getting Close,* by John Ortberg.

The Team: Laura Derico, JamieLyn Heim, Toben Heim,
Verne Kenney, Nick Lee, Wendi Lord, Dave Thornton
Cover Design: Nick Lee with Jacqueline L. Nuñez
Cover Photo: Shutterstock/Ermolaev Alexander
Printed in the United States of America

1 2 3 4 5 6 7 8 9 10

073117

CONTENTS

HOW THIS WORKS

Whether you are a man or a woman; whether you're the life of the party or a wallflower; whether you're a thinker or a feeler or a category not yet known to social science, you were made for connection. You were made for relationships. You were made for intimacy.

Welcome! Whether this is your first time working through a small group study or your thirty-first time, you are sure to have some new experiences here. Some of those experiences will make you feel right at home. And that's a good thing. Some of those experiences may make you feel a little uncomfortable. That's good too. But we don't want to lose you right off the bat, so here's how this thing is meant to work.

Your group will likely have a leader. With any luck, this person will be good at the job, and be someone you can go to if you have any questions. But even if your leader is lost, you don't have to be. Just follow along in this guide—when have we steered you wrong before?

Every time you meet with your group, you'll spend some time getting to know one another and getting to know the subject of the particular session through discussion and group exercises. Check out the Session Menu to get an idea of what to expect.

SESSION MENU

In Group

    Open Up: eat, watch video, talk, pray

    Connect: discuss, do exercises

    Bible Connect: group Bible study

    Go Out: pray and go

Out of Group

    Pray, do exercises, think about questions, reflect on experiences

Here are your responsibilities:

- Participate.
- Listen.
- Be open.

Let's face it—group discussions in which no one talks are extremely painful and awkward—and not the good kind of awkward that we'll talk about later in this book. So be willing to say something. Anything. Share a thought. Ask a question. Comment on someone's answer. Grunt in the affirmative. And if you are one of those people who break out in hives even at the thought of speaking in front of others, know this—you are in the right place. This is a group who cares what you think and how you feel. It's a safe place for you to speak. And who knows? Someone else in your group may also be breaking out in hives—the least you can do is compare spots.

Now, if you are one of those people who could talk all day about anything at all and be thrilled to do it—you are also in the right place. However, try to be aware of the room. Let others speak. Invite others to speak. You don't have to be the leader to lead your fellow group members into the conversation.

So that's part one of this study—In Group. Part two is equally important. But for that, you're on your own. Well, sort of. We hope you'll realize as you go through this guide that you're never on your own. You have a fellow traveler who is always with you, and always ready to hear from you. But even God is not going to fill out this guide and do the exercises for you.

You might be saying at this point—"You mean, we have homework?" Don't worry. There are no hundred-question-long surveys that try to get you to discover if you're more like a seal or a camel. What you've got here is not homework, but life work. There will be some questions to think about, yes. But there will also be stuff to do—challenges to try in your daily life. Little changes to make to your routine. Prayers to pray. Bible verses to discover and rediscover. The opportunity to get to know yourself, your friends, your family, your coworkers, and even strangers a little better. The opportunity to get real about getting close to others and to God.

How and when you complete the Out of Group portion of your session will be up to you. Everyone has different schedules, and your group may be meeting weekly, monthly, or only in leap years. But ideally you'll think through some of the questions and try out some of the exercises before your next group meeting. The benefit to doing that is twofold: first, it will give you something to talk about when you meet next time; second, it may help you realize some questions you have or things you didn't understand about the previous session. Then you can ask those questions in your group and not only get some answers but also help someone else who might be struggling with the same issues.

What else do you need other than this guide and some kind of writing instrument? As you might have guessed by now, there's a bigger book that this guide is a companion to, and if you really want to dig into the topics presented in this study—or if you just want a great read!—you'll want a copy of *I'd Like You More if You Were More like Me: Getting Real about Getting Close* (hereafter referred to as *I'd Like You More*). It's by pastor, speaker, author, and all-around nice guy John Ortberg. In the book he shares some practical, relevant insights about creating connections with others that he has gleaned from decades of ministry and from his own relationships with family and friends. Here's a little glimpse of one such thoughtful reflection:

> I remember one time when we were eating breakfast
> and my mom was holding a piece of peanut butter
> toast. It was that critical peanut-buttering time
> where the toast is still warm enough to melt the
> peanut butter a little, and just as she was lifting the
> toast to her mouth, I reached over and smashed it
> right in her face.

If you're wondering what happened next and how this little episode could possibly have helped the young John form a deep connection with his mother, go get the man's book. You won't be sorry.

You'll also want to have a Bible of some sort available to you. If you're not sure which version to use, check with your pastor, your group leader, or your fellow group members to see what ones they like. Besides print versions, there are many Bible translations available online and via mobile apps.

That's it. You're ready to meet with your group for your first session. But before you do, can we pray for you?

Lord, thank you for the thoughts and gifts and abilities of the person who is now holding this book. Please guide us all into closer, deeper, fuller connection with you and with the people you have placed in our lives. Help us to be open to the experiences, opportunities, and challenges that come with knowing and loving other human beings. Amen.

PREPARE

Do the following before your first session:

- Read the intro and chapters 1 and 2 of *I'd Like You More* (if you have a copy).
- Remember to find a Bible.
- Check with your group leader/host to see if you need to bring any snacks or part of a meal.
- Buckle your seatbelt. It's going to be a wild ride!

AROUND THE TABLE

When I think about love, I think about a table.

IN GROUP

BE PREPARED TO
eat together
talk
draw
laugh
pray

OPEN UP

- Pray.
- Make introductions as needed.
- Make and/or enjoy a meal or snacks together. (The host or leader of the group will provide instructions beforehand for what to bring.)
- Join an icebreaker activity led by the leader.

- Watch the optional video introduction.
- Discuss: What does the image of a family table represent to you?

CONNECT

John Ortberg reflects on how a table has been a symbol of love and relationships in his life: "For the people I grew up with, gathering around a table was the primary love language. If somebody got hurt, got sick, got married, bought a car, bought a house, had a crisis, had a baby, or died, that's what we'd do. There would always be the rich smell of coffee in the house (not Orange Mocha Frappuccino—just coffee), and we'd gather around the table to talk, laugh, and cry—*together*" (*I'd Like You More*).

So many activities in our lives—from the time we are children until we move out of our parents' houses and have tables of our own—take place around tables. We meet at tables to eat together, play cards, or make travel plans. Even in workplaces, people often meet around tables to listen to presentations, discuss ideas, and collaborate on projects. Jesus himself had some pretty interesting life experiences around tables—he even knocked a few over. Though not all these activities involve love, they all are ways of making connections.

Talk about it:

- What memorable experiences with people have you had that took place around a table?
- Who was involved?
- Where did you sit?

- What was it about the table that helped those connections happen?

Easy Group Exercise: Table Talk

Follow the leader's instructions to set up the Table Talk activity.

Think about it:

- What does your seat at your home table look like?
- Is your space at the table big or small? Do you have a lot of influence (take up a lot of space) or not very much?
- Are you quiet or loud around your table?
- Does your space look neat and tidy or loose and busy?
- Is your space at the table shared with others or do you have it all to yourself?

Listen as members of the group describe how they feel about their places at their tables.

> *Of course, the easiest way to keep your table tidy is not to let anyone sit there. But sometimes a table where messy people have spilled creates a memory that a tidy table never could.*

Tables are places where many different people can come together and make connections. It's where relationships can start, grow, and even sometimes where they end. Life at the table can seem predictable and routine, or it can be surprising and unusual.

Whenever people sit and do life together, at some point or another interesting things are bound to happen. And that is just one of the many reasons why some people get uncomfortable at the idea of getting closer to others.

> A table is a reminder that what really matters in life is relationships. We are hardwired for emotional connection to other people. We want to be known. We crave being loved. . . . We crave intimacy.

As Ortberg points out, "Intimacy is a scary concept for a lot of people." And whether we call it intimacy or getting closer or making deeper connections, many people will still have some fears about knowing and being known by others.

Talk about it:
- What are some of those fears people have about getting close?
- What fears do you have?
- Where do these fears come from?

Slightly Awkward Group Exercise: Human Statues

Follow your leader's instructions to break up into pairs and play a unique form of charades.

Think about it:

- Getting in each other's physical space can be uncomfortable and awkward.
- Getting in each other's emotional and spiritual space can be even messier!
- But getting in each other's lives and sharing experiences can be beautiful, funny, and life-changing.

While many of us fear intimacy with others, we wonder even more how in the world we are supposed to achieve intimacy with the almighty, universe-creator, death-defeater God. But God has been pursuing an intimate relationship with us from the very beginning. He is the one who designed us to need and want to be with others.

As we consider how we can create deeper connections with other people and with God, it will be helpful to look more closely at what intimacy is and what it isn't. Ortberg describes these points in detail in his book, but he sums them up pretty well in this statement: "Intimacy is not simply a feeling. It's not a mysterious experience that some people are born for and others are condemned to miss out on. It's not restricted to certain temperaments, or to married couples, or to 'feelers' on the Myers-Briggs continuum. And it's not something that mystically occurs the moment we say, 'I do.'"

Intimacy, Ortberg goes on to say, is sharing experiences—big ones, little ones, everyday ones. It's being present with others in those experiences and allowing time for that to happen. In other words, it's what Jesus did very well. So if we want to dig into what intimacy looks like, we can look at how Jesus interacted with his friends.

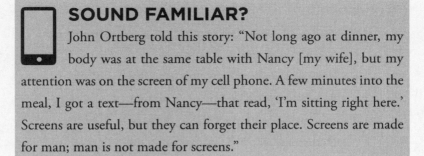

SOUND FAMILIAR?

John Ortberg told this story: "Not long ago at dinner, my body was at the same table with Nancy [my wife], but my attention was on the screen of my cell phone. A few minutes into the meal, I got a text—from Nancy—that read, 'I'm sitting right here.' Screens are useful, but they can forget their place. Screens are made for man; man is not made for screens."

BIBLE CONNECT

Work through some of these questions with your group, but don't feel pressured to talk about them all. Finish any questions you don't get to in your individual time later in the week. If you are short on time, focus on questions 1, 2, and 7–10.

1. Take a look at how Jesus made connections with his disciples. Read Mark 1:16-20 and 2:13-16. Where did Jesus find his first disciples? How would you describe the way he reached out to them? Jewish teachers and leaders normally trained and studied the Scriptures for years, and their students were trained under them. How might Jesus' approach to gathering disciples have seemed in contrast to the traditional way of Jewish teachers?

2. Read Mark 3:13-15. Why did Jesus appoint the Twelve?

3. As we read the Gospels, we can see that the disciples were with Jesus a lot. Go back and reread Mark 1:16-20 and 2:13-16. What were Jesus and his disciples doing together?

4. Find out more about how Jesus and his disciples spent time together. Read Mark 4:33-41. What did Jesus do for the disciples through what he said to them and what he demonstrated in front of them?

5. Part of being intimate with others means knowing them well enough to be able to challenge them. Read Mark 6:30-44. This passage starts out with the disciples coming to Jesus to tell him all that they had done. No doubt they wanted to impress Jesus with the amount of good they had been doing. But Jesus wanted to stretch them some more. What monumental task did he ask them to do?

6. Once again, in Mark 6:45-52, Jesus challenges his friends. They did not understand what he was doing. In the storm on the lake, they didn't even recognize their friend. But Jesus did not give up on them. What did he do?

7. In Mark 8:27-38 we see Jesus having heart-to-heart talks with his disciples about his identity and theirs. What can we learn from those conversations? What does it mean to be close to Jesus? What does it take to follow him?

8. In Mark 10 we find Jesus confiding in his friends. He reveals a key element of developing intimacy with others and with God. Read verses 35-45. What is supposed to be different about those who know and are known by Jesus?

9. In Mark 14:1-42 we see four moving and slightly-awkward portrayals of people demonstrating intimacy with Jesus: the woman with the perfume, Jesus at the Last Supper, Peter with Jesus, and Jesus and his disciples at

Gethsemane. What was moving or emotional about these scenes? What was awkward?

10. Contrast the efforts of the woman with the perfume with those of the disciples in the garden. How do their actions demonstrate intimacy and closeness?

GO OUT

- Pray together.
- Discuss where and when the next meeting will be.
- Exchange contact information as needed.
- Use the space below to jot down a couple thoughts you want to remember and revisit before your next meeting.

_____

_____

_____

_____

_____

OUT OF GROUP

PRAY

As you go through this study, remember to stay in communication with God. Talk to him about your fears and questions. As specific people and relationships come to mind, bring your feelings about those people and experiences to Jesus. If you're ready, ask God to show you opportunities to get closer to specific people in your life.

Slightly Awkward Exercise 1

Ortberg points out how God has been pursuing us from the very beginning. He wants to have an intimate relationship with us. Consider the account in Genesis 3:1-10. When the man and woman ate the fruit, they realized they were naked and hid from God in their shame. God came walking in the garden, looking for Adam and Eve. He was searching for them. He wanted to be with them. So God called out, "Where are you?" (v. 9).

What is your "nakedness"—what are you afraid for God to see? What do you want to hide from God? Take a moment to write down what comes to mind on the figure shown on the next page.

Use your hand to cover the image and hide the words you've written. Now imagine God is walking down your street or down the hallway, just a short distance from where you are sitting right now. And he is calling out to you, "Where are you?" Can you take your hand away and show him what you've been hiding? Whether you are ready to show him or not, talk to him about what you're feeling. Take your time.

. . . .

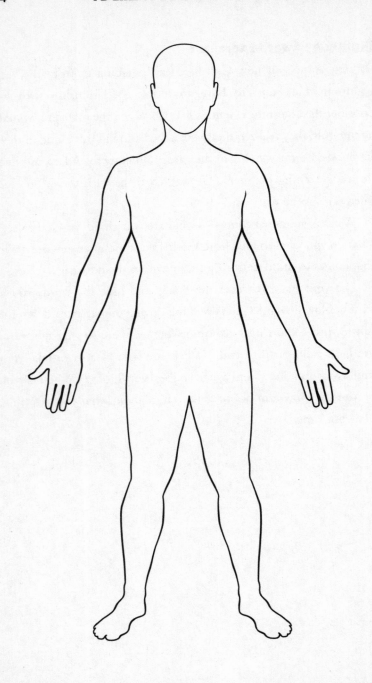

CONNECT AGAIN

Go back and think through the things you did and talked about with your group. Reflect on these things and write about your impressions.

What's something new you learned about the people in your group?

_____

_____

_____

_____

What's something you learned or revisited about yourself?

_____

_____

_____

_____

Pretend the shape on the next page represents the family table in your house when you were growing up. Take some crayons, colored pencils, markers, or other decorations and make this shape represent your feelings about that table from your childhood.

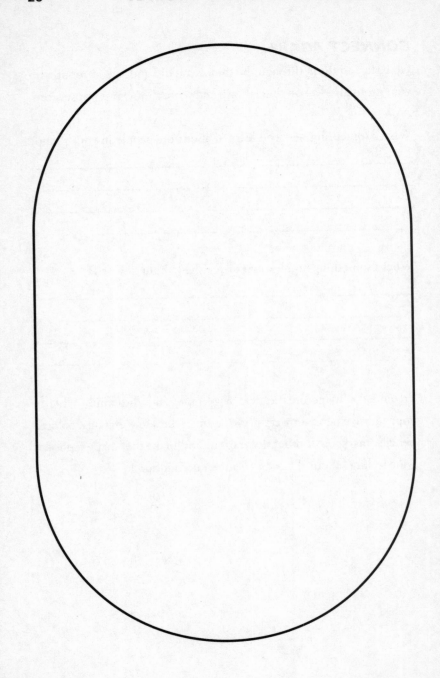

What is one thing you learned about intimacy or connecting with others during your time with your group?

_____

_____

_____

_____

What are some of your fears about getting closer to others?

_____

_____

_____

_____

Slightly Awkward Exercise 2

For many of us, connecting with others will not always come easily. Like most things that are good for us, it's something we have to practice—doing it over and over and over again until it becomes familiar and comfortable. Try practicing making a connection with someone this week. The next time you are waiting in line somewhere, pull out your phone and find a funny, touching, silly, or inspiring image to share with a stranger next to you: it could be a picture of your nephew with his birthday cake or a photo of your dog making a sad face or a silly meme you created. Invite the person next to you: "Since we're stuck here, do you want to see a funny picture of my hamster?" Later, reflect on what about that experience was uncomfortable for you. What felt good? Was it easy or hard for you to do? Why?

· · · · · · · · · ·

As you look at news stories or scroll through Facebook this week, think about how relationships are represented in the media. What do you think intimacy looks like to most people? How is that the same as or different from your own idea of intimacy?

_____

_____

_____

_____

Read through the Bible verses that you talked about with your group. Be sure also to read through any that you didn't have time to discuss in the group. What does intimacy look like to Jesus? How is that the same as or different from your own idea of intimacy?

_____

_____

_____

_____

Ortberg points out several myths about intimacy in his book. One of those is that "Intimacy should be easy." Though you may have an easy time getting close to some people, that isn't going to be true for everyone, and maintaining any relationship takes time and work. What's the state of your relationships right now? Check your intimacy quotient with the following survey.

1. Do you have at least one person on whom you could call in times of personal distress?

___ Yes   ___ No

2. Do you have several people with whom you can visit with little advance warning—without apology?

___ Yes   ___ No

3. Do you have several people with whom you can share recreational activities?

___ Yes   ___ No

4. Do you have people who will lend you money or care for you in practical ways if the need arises?

___ Yes   ___ No

5. How likely are people to come to you when they need help?

___ Very likely   ___ Somewhat likely   ___ Not likely at all

6. Are people willing to be real around you?

___ Definitely   ___ I think so   ___ How would I know?

7. Are you able to have a crucial conversation with your friends about a difference of opinion without losing your sense of connectedness?

___ Absolutely   ___ It depends   ___ Not really

8. Are you comfortable living in disagreement (not anger)
   with someone?
   ___ Totally comfy
   ___ I'm mostly okay with it
   ___ No, I hate it!

9. What do you do when a relationship hits a bump in the
   road?
   ___ Work through it
   ___ Keep going without confronting it
   ___ Abandon the relationship

10. Who might find *you* to be a difficult person?

_____

11. Are you able to be real around others?
    ___ Yes   ___ No   ___ Don't know, haven't tried it

Look back over your answers. How would you describe your experience of intimacy right now in your life?

_____
_____
_____
_____

*(Note: Ortberg offers more questions to go with each of the 11
Intimacy Myths he presents in his book.)*

Everything we've talked about in regards to getting closer to others also applies to our relationship to God. As Ortberg put it, "It's messy, sometimes seasonal, requires time and attention to flourish, is reciprocal by nature, fueled by love, and—here's the big one—it is possible for *everyone*."

This means that the same things that prevent us from building deeper connections with others can also get in the way of our relationship with God: too many distractions, not spending enough quality time together, not being fully present, not doing the work of getting to know him, and not communicating. Answer these questions to check out your current intimacy level with God:

1. How much are you experiencing intimacy with God these days?

   _____

   _____

2. What is your appetite for reading Scripture?

   _____

   _____

3. How naturally do you find yourself experiencing gratitude and expressing it to God?

   _____

   _____

4. Are you praying more or less than you used to?

   _____

   _____

5. Do you find worshipping God with others to be a stress-reliever or a stress-producer? Why?

6. Are you feeling more humble? more patient? more willing
    to give? If not, what do you think is holding you back in
    your growth in these areas?

    _____

    _____

7. When you are connected deeply with God, you care about
    the things God cares about. How often do you notice the
    needs of others and do something in response?

    _____

    _____

Slightly Awkward Exercise 3

Ortberg acknowledged that intimacy is big, "but it's built on small
moments." Do something this week that is small but meaningful for
someone with whom you have a relationship. Give a hug. Bring a
meal or a favorite snack to someone doing taxes, studying for a test,
or trying to get over a sickness. Surprise a person with a caffeinated
beverage on a miserable Monday morning. Or just pay a compli-
ment! Take a photo to capture how you are creating your "small
moment" and share it with your group.

. . . .

PRAY

Pray this prayer based on Philippians 1:9-11:

*God, please help my love for others to grow more and more in knowledge
of them and of you. Give me deep insights so that I can understand what*

is best to do for others and how I can keep my actions pure and blameless. Let me harvest the fruit of Jesus so that all my relationships can bring glory to you. Amen.

PREPARE

Do the following before your next group session:

- Read chapters 3, 4, and 5 of *I'd Like You More* (if you have a copy).
- Have a meal with one or several friends or family members at a table. Put away your screens and ask them to share some of their best memories of times around a table.
- Check your email/text/social media site to see if anyone from your group has posted pics of those "small moments."
- See whether you need to bring any food item to your next group meeting.
- Think about this big question: Why do I crave connection?

CREATED FOR CONNECTION

Vulnerability drives us to intimacy.

IN GROUP

BE PREPARED TO

eat together

talk

sketch

laugh

pray

OPEN UP

- Pray.
- Make and/or enjoy a meal or snacks together. (The host or leader of the group will provide instructions beforehand for what to bring.)
- Join an icebreaker activity led by the leader.

- Watch the optional video introduction.
- Discuss: "The awareness of weakness leads us toward stronger community." Why do you agree or disagree with that statement?

CONNECT

As John Ortberg notes, the need and significance of intimate connections in our lives becomes apparent from the moment we are born: "We hatch to attach" (*I'd Like You More*). For nine months, a baby shares the most intimate physical connection with his or her mother, and then they are separated. And after that separation—right from the start—the mother and father begin to try to understand the baby's requests for connection and to respond appropriately. It's a reflex—a baby cries, a parent soothes. And in that simple interaction, the foundation of identity, security, self-worth, connection, and attachment is laid.

When a baby seeks attention and gets a loving response, that baby takes in a lot of information. She learns that she is a separate person from the person staring back at her. She feels comforted and begins to associate comfort and safety with that person. She learns the difference between being in the presence of her comforter and being alone. She learns that her actions (crying, making noise) produce a consistent effect (someone appears, she gets held, etc.).

But none of this can occur until the baby is out of the womb— the bonding of parent and child can't really begin until there is the separation. It's a process that reflects the very beginnings of life— cells separating, multiplying, and bonding together. It's a process that reflects God's act of creation—separating dark and light, day and night, wet and dry, and so forth, so that he could join them all together to create a flourishing world. It's a process we recreate in a hundred different ways every week without even noticing we are doing it.

Talk about it:

- Talk about a time you've witnessed a baby being soothed (or soothing your own child). What about that interaction is valuable to you?
- What happens when a parent isn't able to soothe the baby right away?
- What is one of the first memories you have of knowing someone cared about you, or of feeling safe when an adult was around?

Easy Group Exercise: Detached Creation

Follow your leader's instructions to join in this interesting artistic exercise.

Think about it:

- What made this exercise not-so-easy?
- Why is it so hard to create something you can't see?
- What did you rely on to help you finish the activity?
- What would have made it easier?

Parents don't always get the attachment thing down right away. Most parents misread their children's cues on a regular basis. Ortberg quoted one study that reported that mothers misunderstood the causes of their babies' distress about 70 percent of the time. But when people are committed to the relationship, they stick with it. They keep trying.

> *In our vulnerability, we run to them, and while we receive the joy of being comforted, they receive the joy of giving comfort.*

Of course, it's not all that surprising to realize that parents don't always understand the needs of their children. They still have trouble understanding one another as they grow up together. And we adults have trouble understanding other adults as well. We don't always communicate clearly. We miss hints. We forget. We ignore. We misinterpret. But in order for our attachment to one another to keep growing, we have to keep trying.

In Chapter 4 of *I'd Like You More*, Ortberg unpacks an idea that relational expert John Gottman calls "bids" for emotional connection: "It turns out that everyone—including you and me—is constantly sending out tiny little probes, emotional nanocrafts. . . . They travel at high speed, and it's easy to miss them. Those who are skillful at recognizing and responding to these probes have a great gift for cultivating intimate friendships. Those who are blind, or nonresponsive to them, often end up alone in the dark."

These tiny probes begin with our infant cries communicating fear, fatigue, hunger, discomfort, or loneliness. But as we develop, these simple cries become questions, comments, looks, touches, facial expressions—anything we send out that is asking someone to notice us, acknowledge us, value us, answer us—to recognize that we are separate persons wanting very much to connect with other persons. We are "I"s that want to be "we"s.

> *Each connection is like a deposit in an emotional bank account.*

Talk about it:

- Have you noticed these bids for intimacy happening in your life? What have you seen?
- Ortberg describes three main ways we can respond to someone's invitation to connect: 1) Accept. 2) Ignore. 3) Reject. What makes you more likely to accept someone's bid? (Consider something as simple as someone asking if you want to join them on a Starbucks run.) What makes you more likely to reject it?

Slightly Awkward Group Exercise: Blind Portraits

For this activity, your group will divide into pairs and follow your leader's instructions. Don't worry—no artistic skill is required for this exercise.

Think about it:
- What did you learn about your partner in this exercise?
- How did you learn those things?
- What, if anything, about performing this activity made you uncomfortable? Why?
- What did you learn about yourself through this exercise?

While we may receive thousands of tiny invitations to connect with others on a daily basis, there is someone else who is both receiving and sending billions of such invitations all the time—God. He's been looking to connect with us since he created us. Sometimes he may make grand invitations through magnificent sunsets on the ocean or the beauty of a misty mountain sunrise. Sometimes he whispers in a still, small voice and sometimes he thunders. Sometimes he gives us a house to build or a cup of water to offer or a hand to hold. Sometimes he just asks us to go for a walk in the garden.

Let's look at how God is inviting us to connect with him through his Word, and think about how we can respond.

SOUND FAMILIAR?

A couple is at a table sharing a meal. They're both looking at their screens, checking Facebook posts and e-mails from work.

"Look at this video of cats playing chess," she says.

He chuckles. Or doesn't. Or grunts. Or shakes his head. Or leans over to take a look.

Depending on how he responds to her bid, he either makes a tiny little intimacy deposit or he doesn't. (from *I'd Like You More*)

BIBLE CONNECT

Work through some of these questions with your group, but don't feel pressured to talk about them all. Finish any questions you don't get to in your individual time before the next session. If you are especially short on time, focus on questions 1, 3, 4, and 7.

1. Skim through chapters 1–3 of Genesis and write down some of the things that God separates and creates or joins together.

2. What good came out of these separations? Was there anything bad that came out of these separations?

3. The themes of separation and reunion appear throughout the story of God's relationship with his people. How do these themes connect to the message of the gospel?

4. "At its core, the gospel is the invitation to an intimate relationship with God" (*I'd Like You More*). How do you think most people respond to that invitation when they hear it? What do you think influences their responses?

5. In the last session, we looked at the way Jesus, the master of intimacy, interacted with his closest friends. Jesus also pursued intimate fellowship with many others, some of whom seemed to be intent on ignoring his invitations. In the Bible a lack of awareness, especially self-awareness, is often compared to blindness or living in the dark. We'll spend the next few questions looking at some who chose

to be blind. First, let's consider poor Martha. Martha's complaint to Jesus regarding her sister is recorded for all time in Luke 10. And so is Jesus' response: "Martha, Martha, you are worried and upset about many things." In what ways was Martha blind to Jesus' invitation?

6. In Luke 12:13-15, a man asks Jesus to resolve a family dispute over an inheritance. But instead of giving financial advice, Jesus warns the man to be on guard against "all kinds of greed." Read these verses and the parable that follows. Talk about a) in what way the man was blind, and b) what Jesus invited him to do instead.

7. Read Luke 6:37-42. How can the kind of blindness represented in these verses be an obstacle to intimacy with others or with God? How could it block you from seeing bids for connection from others?

GO OUT

- Pray together.
- Discuss where and when the next meeting will be.
- Exchange contact information as needed.
- Use the space below to jot down thoughts you want to remember and revisit before your next meeting.

_____

_____

_____

_____

OUT OF GROUP

PRAY

As you go through this study, remember to stay in communication with God. Keep an eye out for specific invitations God may be offering you to connect with him, or opportunities he creates for you to connect with others. Ask God to focus your heart and mind to see these openings and invitations more clearly.

Slightly Awkward Exercise 1

When we are practicing a skill, it can be helpful to track our progress. Use the chart provided here to track bids for connection that you notice before the next group session. Remember that these bids can be subtle: a cashier asks if it is still raining outside, a coworker asks to borrow your phone charger, a friend laments the fact that he has to take his car in for repairs, a spouse asks you to pick up a gallon of milk on the way home. Record the bid, who made it, and how you responded.

BID FOR CONNECTION	WHO MADE IT	HOW I RESPONDED

CONNECT AGAIN

Go back and think through the things you did and talked about with your group. Reflect on these things and write about your impressions.

What's something new you learned about the people in your group?

_____

_____

_____

_____

What's something you learned or revisited about yourself?

_____

_____

_____

_____

Consider what you've learned about how we were designed for connection and about how that design shows up in the way we act, even from birth. Either from your own experience or from what you've seen in other families, list some of the positive effects that come from attachment. Then list some of the negative results that come from attachment disorder, which develops when parents do not respond appropriately to the needs of their children.

POSITIVE EFFECTS	NEGATIVE RESULTS

How does being aware of your need for intimacy affect your attitude about pursuing connections with others?

_____

_____

_____

_____

How do you think being more aware of yourself—of who you are, how you were designed, what you want, what you need, and how you feel—could help you pursue deeper connections with the people closest to you? How might this self-awareness also produce fears that could block you from pursuing connections with others? What can you do to get rid of those obstacles?

_____

_____

_____

_____

_____

_____

_____

_____

Slightly Awkward Exercise 2

Use the provided chart to record the bids for connection that you send out to others. As you keep track of these bids, remember that sending and responding to bids for connection is something everyone is practicing all the time—the only man who mastered it was Jesus. If your bids are ignored or rejected, consider all the aspects of why that might have happened. Don't turn this into a bitterness chart!

BID FOR CONNECTION	WHO WAS IT FOR?	WHAT WAS THE RESPONSE?

Read through the Bible verses that you talked about with your group. Be sure also to read through any that you didn't have time to discuss. Think about how the gospel is an invitation to relationship with God. How have you responded to that invitation in the past? How are you responding to it today? What has affected your response?

_____

_____

_____

_____

_____

_____

_____

_____

Consider the kinds of blindness presented in the Bible and discussed by your group. Have you been afflicted by some kind of spiritual blindness? What is clouding your vision?

_____

_____

_____

_____

One of the tricky parts of pursuing deeper connections with others is the need to be aware of the person you are connecting with, and how he or she affects you and your relationships with others or with God. This is where practicing self-awareness becomes crucial. In Chapter 5 of *I'd Like You More*, Ortberg talks about the self that is elicited through our relationships with others. Each person in our lives either pulls us toward or away from our best selves. Think of some of the people in your life with whom you spend the most time. As you think of each one, ask yourself: How does my connection with this person have an impact on who I'm becoming?

_____

_____

_____

_____

_____

_____

_____

Of course, Jesus is not only the master of intimacy, but he's also the master of eliciting our best selves. What can you do this week to spend more time connecting with Jesus?

_____

_____

_____

_____

Slightly Awkward Exercise 3

We don't just send and receive bids for connection to and from other people every day; we also are always being offered opportunities to connect with our Father, God. Use this chart to record specific times when you recognized God was offering you an opportunity to connect with him, then record how you responded.

ONLINE ACCESS PASS

Thank you for choosing *I'd Like You More if You Were More like Me Small Group Connection Kit*. We are excited for you to learn how to connect on a deeper level with the people God has placed in your life, both inside and outside your small group, as together you grow closer to the One who made us for relationships.

ACCESS THE VIDEOS

Step 1:   Go to *GetRealGetClose.com/groupresources* and follow the on-screen directions.

Step 2:   Use the password **GETCLOSE** when prompted.

You now have access to all the videos for this curriculum!

If you have any questions or problems accessing these resources, please contact one of our ministry consultants at 800.323.7543 or email *customercare@davidccook.com*.

I'D LIKE YOU MORE IF YOU WERE MORE LIKE ME

SHARE EXPERIENCES. BREAK DOWN BARRIERS. CREATE CONNECTIONS.

Whether this is your first time working through a small group study or your thirty-first time, you are sure to have some new experiences here.

Loving one another well can get difficult, messy, and just plain awkward. You and your small group will learn together to move past the fear of close relationships and to the joy of everyday connections. With helpful tips, motivating quotes, easy-to-lead discussion questions, and simple exercises, this study will encourage you to embrace the awkwardness and engage everyone in the challenge to get real about getting closer to God and one another.

Brief videos are available to begin each session, featuring pastor and author, John Ortberg. His compelling stories and encouraging words will provide a great atmosphere for launching into exploration of God's plan for relationships.

GOD'S BID FOR CONNECTION	WHEN?	HOW DID I RESPOND?

PRAY

As a metaphor for achieving self-awareness and getting rid of the obstacles that keep us from connecting with Jesus, John Ortberg refers to the story C. S. Lewis wrote of a boy named Eustace. Eustace was turned into a dragon, and Aslan the lion invited the boy to be remade. Ask Jesus to remove your dragon skin as you pray:

Jesus, thank you for providing a way for me to have an intimate relationship with you. Remove all my defensiveness, denial, and self-justification. Remove my pride and my fear. Open my eyes and make me see the truth about myself—and my sin. Even if it hurts me for a while, Lord, strip away any layers of falsehood I have built up to make myself look better in front of others. Help me to see myself as who you created me to be, as a child who wants to be attached to you. Purify my thoughts and help me identify my feelings. Give me the desire to belong to you wholly. Thank you for the free gift of grace that makes that possible. Amen.

PREPARE

Do the following before your next group session:

- Read chapters 6 and 7 of *I'd Like You More* (if you have a copy).
- Make sure to fill in your "bids for connection" charts.
- Consider using the hashtag #GodBid to post or tweet about times you noticed God inviting you to connect.
- Find out if you need to bring any food item to your next group meeting.
- Think about this big question: Can the idea of misery loving company ever be a good thing?

COMPASSION AND COMMITMENT

It's not a bad thing to be an admirer of his. But he's looking for disciples.

IN GROUP

BE PREPARED TO

eat together

talk

remember

rejoice

mourn

pray

OPEN UP

- Pray.
- Make and/or enjoy a meal or snacks together. (The host or leader of the group will provide instructions beforehand for what to bring.)

- Join an icebreaker activity led by the leader.
- Watch the optional video introduction.
- Discuss: Have you ever had a time when sharing with others in a (typically considered) negative activity turned into a positive, community-building moment? What happened?

CONNECT

In Chapter 6 of *I'd Like You More*, John Ortberg says, "The core secret to human connection is found in a single command given by the apostle Paul. If you follow this principle, you will never lack for intimate friendships. If you fail to follow it, you will never experience intimate relationships. . . . This principle is so simple that even a child can master it, and so challenging that even some geniuses never quite get it. What is the golden rule of intimacy? Here it is: 'Rejoice with those who rejoice; mourn with those who mourn'" (Romans 12:15).

Our ability to develop deep connections with others hangs on our ability to listen to, to watch for signs of, and to notice feelings—particularly the feelings of the other person (we're often pretty good at noticing our own). We can only share in someone's experience of joy or mourning if we are aware that they are having that experience. But awareness is not enough. We have to go one step further and not just act as a shoulder to cry on or wave a victory flag—we have to feel *with* the person. He cries, we cry (or in the case of the less teary among us, at least make a sad face and provide some tissues). She shouts for joy, we shout for joy (or again, for the quieter voices among us, we at least need to come up with a grin and a high five).

It may be helpful (especially later when we look at the book of Psalms) to think about this kind of active compassion as singing a song with a choir. Imagine the strange looks you'd get if you sang along with the upbeat, cheerful tune everyone else was singing (think "Jesus Loves Me"), but you chose a depressing minor key. Likewise, if everyone was singing a sorrowful requiem, you wouldn't dare slap on a cheesy grin and bounce about as if you were warbling "Happy Birthday"—at least, not unless you secretly wanted to get kicked out of your choir robe.

An act of compassion requires just that—acting as though *you* are the one who is suffering loss or being granted joy. It's an act of powerful imagination—using your own experiences to help you share in someone else's. And that makes it an act of intimacy.

Talk about it:

- Describe a time when you had a problem singing the same tune as others—either in rejoicing or mourning. What happened? Why was it difficult for you?

- Ortberg remarks that sharing joy increases joy and sharing pain decreases pain. What do you think about that? Would you agree or disagree?

- Consider a time when you were guilty of rejoicing when someone else was mourning. Why did that happen? (Keep in mind *mourning* here just means any sad experience: from dropping an ice cream cone to losing your whole ice cream truck business. Although those would be equally sad events, for sure.)

- Describe a time when you felt sad that someone else was experiencing joy. (Just think back to the most recent government elections of any significance in your region, and you'll probably be able to come up with some examples.) What would be good reasons for feeling that way?

Easy Group Exercise: Valley/Peak Moments

Follow your leader's instructions to use a whiteboard or a large poster board to record the valley and peak moments of your group from the last week.

Think about it:

- Who celebrates everyday victories and frustrations with you?
- If you don't share either of these things regularly, why not? What keeps you from telling someone about your experiences and how you feel about them?
- What role do trust and commitment play when you choose people with whom you can share experiences?

A good listener understands facts. An intimate listener understands feelings.

Sharing experiences of suffering or joy can make even strangers feel more bonded to each other. Joy tends to be contagious—which may be why we are commanded in the Bible to be joyful. Joy enhances the life of everyone in earshot. Have you ever witnessed someone who really enjoys her job? She spreads joy to everyone on staff—increasing the productivity and the morale of the whole company.

But what about mourning? What is the good in mourning together? The good there comes in the "together." Mourning with others means you take some of their burdens and carry them for a little while. "Mourning with" does not mean fixing problems, quoting scriptural hopefulness, or trying to get someone else to stop mourning. It means grieving, being sad. It means just sitting with a fellow human in his sorrow and letting him know he is not alone.

Tears are one of God's most brilliant intimacy inventions.

Talk about it:

- Have you ever had a hard time expressing your feelings in front of others? What happened?
- What makes it easier or harder for you to express your feelings to people with whom you have established, committed relationships?
- How can sharing in such experiences regularly create an atmosphere where commitment can happen?

Slightly Awkward Group Exercise:
Valley/Peak Life Graphs

Follow your leader's instructions to break up into pairs and talk about your valley and peak life experiences.

Think about it:

- The person you are and the life you lead are shaped by your valley and peak experiences.
- Your relationship with God can be affected by your valley and peak experiences.
- Sharing these experiences with others can help you find common ground where you think none exists.

Sharing in meaningful experiences with one another not only helps us relate to each other in the moment, but it also tests our trust of one another. *After I tell them about this, will they stay? Will they want to be with me even after the rejoicing is over?*

Commitment is the foundation of intimacy, because without commitment there can be no trust, and without trust, there can be no intimacy.

When we trust someone and commit to being that person's friend, spouse, business partner, parent, or 5K teammate, we create a space where we are free to share in more—and deeper—experiences. Those commitments also reflect our relationship with God. We are made in the image of a vowing, faithful, covenant-making God, who has created us for connection and who promises not to disconnect from us.

But commitment does come with certain costs. Ortberg refers to a description of these costs, as written by Lew Smedes: a loss of control, a loss of individuality, and a loss of freedom. However, Ortberg also notes that "commitment leads to a deeper freedom than all the other options and escape clauses in a commitment-phobic world" (*I'd Like You More*).

SOUND FAMILIAR?

Only human beings can make a promise. . . . Only human beings can say, "I will meet you next Tuesday. I will serve on that team with you. I will keep that secret. I will be your friend. I will pray for you. I will have your back. You can count on me." Dogs can't make that promise. If they could, they would—and they would die to keep it—but they can't. Cats can't make that promise. If they could, they would, and then they would break it, and they would laugh in your face in their quiet cat way. (from *I'd Like You More*)

BIBLE CONNECT

Work through some of these questions with your group, but don't feel pressured to talk about them all. Finish any questions you don't get to in your individual time before the next session. If you are short on time, focus on questions 1, 2, 5, and 7.

1. If we want to have some practice rejoicing and mourning with others, we can find no better place than the book of Psalms. Read Psalm 23, where both joy and sorrow are

represented. This psalm is often associated with mournful events such as the passing of loved ones—it is often read at funerals. But take a closer look. Write down all the imagery in this psalm that represents contentment or joy or gratitude. Now write down all the imagery that reflects sorrow or mournful times. How would you describe the main focus of this psalm?

2. The shortest verse in the Bible is also one of the most powerful: "Jesus wept" (John 11:35). Read verses 11-37 and discuss why Jesus was so moved at this time. What does that tell us about Jesus? What does that tell us about mourning with others?

3. Read Psalm 95:1-7. What images does the psalmist use to express joy in his writing? Is he expecting to rejoice on his own?

4. Think about the kind of commitments God has made to his people. Read Genesis 15. What promises does God make to Abram in these verses? What did God do to show that he would keep his promises?

5. Now look at the kinds of commitments we should make to God. Read the story of Elijah and Elisha from 1 Kings 19:19-21. Elijah at this point is an old, tired, penniless prophet. From the text we see that Elisha is healthy and wealthy—he had twelve yoke of oxen! How does Elisha respond to Elijah when Elijah offers him his cloak (symbolizing his offer of the job of prophet to Elisha)? What does Elisha give up to go with Elijah? What does this show

about Elisha's commitment to Elijah and to God? How would you describe his commitment?

6. Read about Jonathan and David's friendship in 1 Samuel 18:1-4; 19:1-7; 20. What did Jonathan risk for David? What did David risk? What promises did they make to each other?

7. Read Luke 9:23-25. What kind of commitment is Jesus talking about in these verses? How would you describe that commitment?

GO OUT

- Pray together.
- Discuss where and when the next meeting will be.
- Exchange contact information as needed.
- Use the space below to jot down what you want to remember and revisit before your next meeting.

_____

_____

_____

_____

OUT OF GROUP

PRAY

As you go through this study, remember to stay in communication with God. Thank God for the promises he has made to you. Thank him for the people in your life who rejoice and mourn with you. Ask him to show you the parts of your life where you are living as if you are not committed to him.

Slightly Awkward Exercise 1

Like other actions in this study, rejoicing and mourning with others won't necessarily come naturally to you. Practice rejoicing and mourning with others—even people you may not immediately feel happy or sorry for. When you are standing in line at the grocery or a convenience store, check out the headlines on the tabloid news or on magazine covers. Instead of feeling contempt or dismay toward the people featured, consider what it must be like to be involved in their lives. Put yourself in the shoes of the celebrities who are going through divorces, dealing with public revelations about their health issues, or having other intimate details of their lives put on display. Mourn with them in the stresses and pressures they are enduring. Rejoice over good news of good box office sales or awards.

CONNECT AGAIN

Go back and think through the things you did and talked about with your group. Reflect on these things and write about your impressions.

As you talked about each other's valley and peak moments, what's something new you learned about the people in your group?

_____

_____

_____

_____

What's something you learned or revisited about yourself? What did you learn from charting your peaks and valleys throughout your life?

_____

_____

_____

_____

During your time with your group in the last session, what is one thing you learned about intimacy or connecting with others? What increases intimacy? On what is intimacy built?

_____

_____

_____

_____

_____

Name one thing that keeps you from rejoicing or mourning with others. What can you do to get rid of this obstacle?

_____

_____

_____

_____

Fill out the provided chart to represent what you've experienced this week. On the first row, draw or write something to represent your main feeling about that day (happy, sad, angry, frustrated, confused, etc.). Then fill in the other rows with some details to say why that day was a peak or valley kind of day.

	SUN	MON	TUE	WED	THU	FRI	SAT
Your feelings							
^ or v ? Peak or valley?							
Who shared your experience with you?							

Slightly Awkward Exercise 2

Every day for the next five days, do this: As soon as you wake up, write down five simple things for which you are grateful. Record your lists here.

DAY 1	DAY 2	DAY 3	DAY 4	DAY 5
1.	1.	1.	1.	1.
2.	2.	2.	2.	2.
3.	3.	3.	3.	3.
4.	4.	4.	4.	4.
5.	5.	5.	5.	5.

Read through the Bible verses that you talked about with your group. Be sure also to read through any that you didn't have time to discuss in the group. If you have time, read more of the psalms. Jot down any interesting words or phrases that represent rejoicing or mourning.

_____

_____

_____

_____

Consider either something that you were happy about lately (new job, favorite team won the big game, son got all As, etc.) or something that you were sad or frustrated about (lost your favorite pen, didn't get the promotion you wanted, family goldfish died). Write your own psalm of celebration or of lamentation, expressing your feelings about this event. Jot down some ideas on these lines. Post your psalm somewhere where your group can see it.

_____

_____

_____

_____

_____

_____

_____

Read Luke 9:23-25. What do you think these verses mean? What kind of commitment are you willing to make to Jesus right now?

_____

_____

_____

_____

_____

_____

Slightly Awkward Exercise 3

Assess your commitment levels for different roles that you currently hold. Which roles do you find yourself asking these questions about?

1. How little can I do and still be called a _____?
   (Fill in the blank with a role you hold: good coach, good husband, good teacher, good supervisor, good mom, etc.)
2. How much longer do I have to do this?
3. Do I have to do this?

Which roles do you find yourself making these statements about?

1. I wonder how I can be a better _____.
   (Fill in the blank with a role you hold.)
2. I hope I get to do this forever.
3. It's my honor to do this.

If you have any roles that fall into the top category, what do you think you need to do to either change those roles or to change your attitude about them?

· · · · · · · · · ·

PRAY

John Ortberg tells how he once heard Dallas Willard give this advice in answer to someone who wanted to know how to grow spiritually: "Do the next right thing." Pray this prayer, asking God to help you do the next right thing.

God, please help me to see the next thing you have for me to do. And when I see it, help me to do it—even if it is difficult, or awkward, or annoying. Help me to work harder on the projects that I dislike. Help me to encourage people even when I don't feel encouraged. Help me to notice others and speak to them even when I don't feel like talking. Help me to use kind words when I'm frustrated. Help me to be patient with everyone. Help me to apologize first. I know I can't do these things on my own, Lord. Please help me. Amen.

PREPARE

Do the following before your next group session:

- Read chapters 8 and 9 of *I'd Like You More* (if you have a copy).
- Consider any commitments or promises that you have broken. What (if anything) can you do to make amends?
- Check your email/text/social media site to see if anyone has posted the psalms they wrote.
- Find out if you need to bring any food item to your next group meeting.
- Think about this big question: What walls have I built between myself and others?

WALLS AND CRACKS

Intimacy goes up when walls come down.

IN GROUP

BE PREPARED TO
eat together

talk

build

laugh

pray

OPEN UP

- Pray.
- Make and/or enjoy a meal or snacks together. (The host or leader of the group will provide instructions beforehand for what to bring.)
- Join an icebreaker activity led by the leader.
- Watch the optional video introduction.

- Discuss: How does the idea of fully revealing all your faults, sins, and weaknesses to someone make you feel? Does it appeal to you or does it make you want to run away? Why?

CONNECT

"Our world is a world of walls," Ortberg notes in Chapter 8 of *I'd Like You More*. He talks about tangible walls and invisible walls of the heart. The walls of the heart are much harder to scale. Perhaps that is because the walls we put up around ourselves are specifically built to keep others out. As Ortberg puts it: "My ego blinds me to walls. My ego whispers to me that I am entitled to my life of privilege. It blinds me to the humanity of the kids across the counter at McDonald's, the person who takes my money at the gas station, the Vietnamese woman at Supercuts who cuts my hair."

When we build walls between ourselves and others we blind ourselves to our similarities and make it difficult, if not impossible, to make any kind of connections.

In *I'd Like You More*, Ortberg describes in detail different kinds of walls and the problems they produce—there are many stories and examples to explore. But in general, the problems all boil down to these four issues:

- Walls make me more disconnected.
- Walls make me more isolated.
- Walls make me lose perspective.
- Walls make me too comfortable with walls.

Talk about it:

- Have you ever felt like you were placed outside someone's wall? What was that like?
- What kinds of walls have you erected around yourself, and why?
- Be honest. Do you like your walls? Explain.

Easy Group Exercise: Build a Wall

Follow the leader's instructions to set up and participate in the Build a Wall activity.

Think about it:

- Think back to your childhood. What were the first walls you can remember experiencing?
- Why do you think people build walls?
- What do you think about this statement: "When we are connected to life and to each other, we thrive. When we are disconnected, we die"?

As you build a wall together, consider the difference between building a purposeful wall with people and building a wall by yourself.

It's not the achievements, but the intimate moments of our lives that we remember.

Walls tend to represent strength in our culture, yet so often they are built as a result of fear. "We have to keep them out." "We can't let them get us." "We've got to protect our borders."

But God is the one who breaks down our walls—sometimes literally, as in the case of Jericho, when Joshua and his men marched around and around the city and the walls came tumbling down through the power of the Almighty. But more often God breaks down those walls around our hearts so that we can become vulnerable to him. When we are weak, he is strong.

God created us in his image. So, he gave us authority over all the earth. But he also created us to be utterly dependent on him. Naked. As Ortberg points out, "Our lives begin and end in vulnerability." And when God became man his life began and ended the same way—laid in a manger as an infant with the blood of birth wiped away, then laid in the tomb as a man with the blood of death wiped away.

> *We see the ultimate combination of vulnerability and authority in Jesus. . . . And this enables him to offer us ultimate intimacy.*

Talk about it:

- What fears do you have about becoming vulnerable to others?
- Where do those fears come from?
- What fears do you have about becoming vulnerable to God?

Slightly Awkward Group Exercise: Kryptonite

Follow your leader's instructions to engage in this activity about weaknesses and strengths.

Think about it:

- We often make the assumption that if we reveal our weaknesses to someone, that person might use the information against us. But God wants to use our weaknesses to make us stronger.
- Think about when your childhood fears started. What was happening at that time? What things contributed to these fears?
- How hard is it for you to believe that God can bring strength out of your weaknesses? Why?

Through breaking down our walls (or letting God tear them down) and embracing our vulnerability, we can become more like Christ. And in becoming more like Christ, we can get closer to achieving real, true intimacy with God and with each other.

SOUND FAMILIAR?

In a series of studies published in *Science*, researchers gave subjects a choice: sit alone with your thoughts for six to fifteen minutes or give yourself an electric shock. *One-fourth* of the women—and *two-thirds* of the men—chose the shock. One man shocked himself *190 times* in fifteen minutes. Some people would rather punish themselves with electric pain than be still. (from *I'd Like You More*)

BIBLE CONNECT

Work through some of these questions with your group, but don't feel pressured to talk about them all. Finish any questions you don't get to in your individual time later in the week. If you are short on time, focus on questions 5-8.

1. When we consider whether or not we should keep our walls, it may be good to look at Ephesians 2:11-22. What kind of wall is mentioned? Whom or what does the wall divide? What words would you pick out to illustrate God's desire concerning that wall?

2. Instead of being divided by a wall, what are the two groups in Ephesians 2 being joined and built together to become?

3. What does verse 18 assure us that we have?

4. We've learned that we are created for connection. In trying busily to feed that need for connection, we can get sucked into technology (phones, Internet, social media) to the extent that we actually build more walls—isolating ourselves from real people, face-to-face conversations, and physical touch. Technology can never satisfy our need for connection. Look at Psalm 139 to see how God satisfies that need instead. Write down what we can know about our Lord from what we read in verses 1, 2, 4, and 7-10.

5. The story of Jacob features both the struggle to find balance between authority and vulnerability and the kinds of walls that get built when pride and greed and insecurity dominate a relationship. Read about the beginning of

Jacob's life in Genesis 25:21-28. What can you know about Jacob from this glimpse of his life? What kind of wall do you see being built between Jacob and his brother even early in their lives?

6. Read Genesis 27. What further building is done on the walls between Jacob and Esau in this chapter? Write down any words or phrases that create a picture of the kind of relationship that existed between the brothers, or between either of the sons and their parents.

7. Read Genesis 29:15-35. In what ways does the story of Rachel and Leah reflect some of the themes in the story of Jacob and Esau? What fears shaped the actions Leah took?

8. Though the story of Jacob is filled with betrayal, dishonesty, hurt, and struggle, his story comes full circle in Genesis 32 and 33, when Jacob returns and must meet his brother Esau—the twin brother he has not seen since he betrayed Esau and ran away. Jacob is anxious (naturally) about meeting Esau. Read Genesis 33:1-11 to see what happened when they met. How did Esau greet his brother? Who was vulnerable in this scene? Who held authority?

GO OUT

- Pray together.
- Discuss where and when the next meeting will be.
- Exchange contact information as needed.

- Use the space below to jot down a couple thoughts you want to remember and revisit before your next meeting.

_____

_____

_____

_____

OUT OF GROUP

PRAY

As you go through this study, remember to stay in communication with God. Go to him with your questions about vulnerability, authority, and intimacy. Talk to him about walls you've built up between you and others. If you're ready, ask God to show you opportunities to get closer to specific people and how to tear down the walls that are getting in the way of reconciliation. Talk to him about healthy boundaries as well, and how to know the difference between a wall that is truly protecting you and one that is just blocking beneficial relationships.

Slightly Awkward Exercise 1

As you start your personal study time, read the first line of Psalm 46:10. Meditate on this statement by reading it over and over, removing a word or two each time as shown below. As you read the line each time, imagine that God is commanding you to be still. Think about what it means to be still in your busy life. It might mean: *Be still and don't answer that text.* Or it might mean: *Be still, the dishes will wait.* Or it might mean: *Be still; don't worry about the news headlines.* Or it might mean: *Be still; let me heal your anxious heart today.* Think about what it means to know that God is the one true God. As you leave the stillness of this place, consider how you might carry the stillness with you through the day—maybe by stilling angry thoughts in traffic or by stilling your tongue and not gossiping. Or maybe you take the stillness and knock something off your schedule today and spend more time with family instead. Consider how you can use stillness and the knowledge of who God is to improve one part of your day.

> Be still and know that I am God.
> Be still and know that I am.
> Be still and know.
> Be still.
> Be.

· · · · · · · · · ·

CONNECT AGAIN

Go back and think through the things you did and talked about with your group. Reflect on these things and write about your impressions.

What's something new you learned about the people in your group?

_____

_____

_____

_____

What's something you learned or revisited about yourself?

_____

_____

_____

_____

Consider the different kinds of walls you may have around you. Draw or write about those walls below. Give a brief history of how they came to be. Explain what you think your walls are blocking out.

_____

_____

_____

_____

What is something new you learned about connecting with others? What do you think about the idea of vulnerability being necessary for intimacy?

_____

_____

_____

_____

Slightly Awkward Exercise 2

Take this technology-use assessment and give it to someone else as well. So many of us use technology, either intentionally or unwittingly, as a wall to block interactions with actual people, face-to-face. Evaluate your technology usage and see where you might need to make some changes.

1. Do you sleep with your cell phone on your nightstand or in your bed?

2. Do your friends or does your spouse complain about you attending to a screen too much?

3. Do you check your phone first thing in the morning and last thing at night?

4. Do you feel bummed when you forget to bring your cell phone into the bathroom?

5. Do you feel anxious if you don't have Internet access for any period of time?

6. Have you practiced the art of secretly texting while maintaining eye contact?

7. Do you check your cell phone during business meetings, intimate dinners, or sermons?

8. Has anyone ever called you a phone/tech/screen addict?

If you answered yes to a majority (or all) of these, you may have a tech addiction problem. The good news is, you're not alone. But the bad news is, you're not alone. The thing about developing intimacy in your relationships means that you actually need to be present with one another—not just warm bodies in the same room. It means eye contact. It means focused attention for more than thirty seconds. So practice detaching from the phone this week and instead attaching to a person. Each time you are going to be someplace where you will need to interact with people—entering your office building, having dinner, talking to the drive-thru attendant—put your phone facedown on a surface and remove your hands from it, or put it into a pocket or purse. Put the phone away. Look people in the eye and smile or nod. Listen. Then after the interactions are finished, you may touch your phone again.

If you don't think you really look at your phone that much, get some of those small star stickers or yard sale price dot stickers. Every time you reach for your phone or look at your phone (other than when you are making or answering an actual necessary phone call or text), put a sticker on the back of it. If, by the end of the day, your phone is covered with stickers, you may need to make some changes.

· · · · · · · · · ·

What other habits or routines do you have that might be blocking interactions with people? Think about what your average day looks like. What's one small change you could make that might allow you to have more time to notice and act on someone's bid for connection with you?

_____

_____

_____

_____

Read through the Bible verses that you talked about with your group. Be sure also to read through any of the questions that you didn't have time to discuss. What did you learn about God's perspective on walls?

_____

_____

_____

_____

Read Ephesians 2:18. What does it mean to you to have access to God? Is that something you welcome or do you feel a little afraid to approach God? Explain the reasons for your feelings.

_____

_____

_____

_____

Read Matthew 25:34-40. What do you think about this statement: "Jesus is most present in the most vulnerable"?

_____

_____

_____

_____

Slightly Awkward Exercise 3

In the stories of Jacob and Esau and Rachel and Leah, we see that Jacob's interactions with his brother and father meant that he felt identified as Not-Esau. In a similar way, Leah must have felt identified as Not-Rachel. Feeling that you are defined in comparison to someone else—and that you fall short—puts a strain on relationships. But identifying that feeling is the first step toward healing.

Think about your relationships with family, friends, or coworkers. Do you feel like you are identified as Not-Someone? With what word or name would you replace "someone"?

Mentally remove from yourself the Not-Someone name tag. Instead, envision a tag that says, "I am _____." Fill in the blank with positive qualities that you display or beneficial roles that you play.

. . . .

PRAY

Pray this prayer based on verses from Psalm 139:

Lord, search me and know me. Know all my ways. Hear my words before they reach my tongue. No matter where I go or how far I go, Lord, guide me with your hand. I praise you because I am fearfully and wonderfully made. Know my heart, Lord. Know what makes me anxious. Lead me in the way that is not wrapped up in things that don't matter, Lord. Lead me in your way that leads to everlasting life. Amen.

PREPARE

Do the following before your next session:

- Read chapters 10, 11, and 12 of *I'd Like You More* (if you have a copy).
- Remember to take the tech assessment, and practice putting your screen down to allow for more interactions with actual people.
- Find out if you need to bring any food item to your next group meeting.
- Think about this big question: Does sharing in suffering always lead to greater intimacy?

WOUNDS AND HEALING

We need an acceptance that's bigger than our rejections.

IN GROUP

BE PREPARED TO

eat together

talk

be in the dark

laugh

pray

OPEN UP

- Pray.
- Make and/or enjoy a meal or snacks together. (The host or leader of the group will provide instructions beforehand for what to bring.)
- Join an icebreaker activity led by the leader.
- Watch the optional video introduction.

- Discuss: What impact does sharing together in suffering have on relationships? Explain.

CONNECT

In this session we'll be talking about several big themes: suffering and hope, rejection and acceptance, rupture and repair. Though some of the wounds we will discuss happen at the hands of humans and some just happen, two things are true: they all sting and they all leave scars.

But what determines if suffering, rejection, or ruptures will lead to deeper connections with others or lead to isolation? What determines if our story ends in redemption or destruction? No matter the source of our pain, the outcome is largely up to us. How we come out of suffering and what we gain from it depends on our ability to meet God in the middle of it and hold on to others through it.

Talk about it:

- We have a tendency to want to create an inspirational story out of every tale of suffering. But sometimes suffering just causes damage. Talk about a time when something bad happened and there did not seem to be a silver lining.

- John Ortberg refers to *The Deep Down Dark*, the story of 33 Chilean miners who were trapped for 69 days. He then goes on to use that phrase as a metaphor for the place of suffering. In his description of what happened to the miners, he remarks, "They were at their best when life was at its worst." Can you think of a deep down dark experience you've had or have heard about where that was true—where people were at their best when something terrible had happened? Describe that experience. Why do you think people were able to be at their best?

Easy Group Exercise: Cheer Up

Follow the leader's instructions to set up and participate in this activity in which you'll try to get smiles out of your "sufferers."

Think about it:

- This was just a silly game, but have you ever had the experience of someone trying to make you happy at a time when you were not feeling happy? How did the other person's efforts make you feel?
- What do you think: Is it better to try to make someone feel good or better to just listen to how they are feeling?

"Suffering changes people." This is something we hear often, and no doubt it is always true to some degree, depending on the severity of the suffering. But exactly how we change through suffering and how others deal with those changes determine how well our relationships survive. Ortberg discusses three ways that intimacy can build through suffering: by honoring differences, learning how best to respond to people who are suffering, and giving lots of patience.

If we want to see how to both deal with suffering and with sufferers well, we have an example in the Man of Sorrows. About him,

Ortberg says: "On the cross, [Jesus] chose to *share* in the experiences that most isolate us—guilt, pain, hopelessness, and death. And the mysterious result is that we no longer have to be alone—or afraid— in those moments" (*I'd Like You More*).

Suffering with *is an act of tremendous intimacy.*

Some kinds of suffering we seem to bring on ourselves—through trying things and failing or not trying things for fear of failure. "We try out for teams we don't make; we apply for jobs we don't get; we pitch projects we can't sell. We don't wear clothes we love because we're afraid we'll look silly; we don't offer to use gifts God has given us because we're afraid we'll get turned down" (*I'd Like You More*).

When we experience rejection we may react in many different ways, from sorrow to anger to disappointment to eating ice cream. But probably the most damaging reaction to rejection we suffer is the feeling of shame. Shame takes root deep inside us and affects the way we look at ourselves. It is the condemning of self, by the self. It makes us feel that we will never be acceptable, that we will never be accepted.

Guilt causes us to feel bad about what we've done; *shame causes us to feel bad about* who we are.

Healing from that kind of suffering can come—we see it come in the story of the Samaritan woman. A woman who had been shaped by her life choices came to the well and drew up a bucket of transformation. Or as Ortberg puts it: "This is a woman who came to the well with a bucket and went home with the well." And that same living water that refreshed her soul and renewed her heart is the same living water we can drink from today. It's the same water that brings us this revelation: "Therefore, there is now no condemnation for those who are in Christ Jesus, because through Christ Jesus the law of the Spirit who gives life has set you free from the law of sin and death" (Romans 8:1, 2). No condemnation. Not from others. Not from yourself. Not from God.

Talk about it:

- Think back to when you were a small child. When was the first time you remember feeling ashamed?
- How did that shame go away? (Or did it?)
- Talk about a recent rejection that you suffered. Whether it was big or small in your eyes, why did it bother you? How did suffering that rejection affect your relationships?

Slightly Awkward Group Exercise: Shattered

Follow your leader's instructions as you think about repairing ruptures.

Think about it:

- Some ruptures in relationships are worse than others. What kinds of issues are hard for you to get over?

- Ortberg asks this question in *I'd Like You More*: "Is it really possible to have honest conflict and still remain connected?" How would you answer that question?

> *Every relationship experiences ruptures from time to time. What determines ongoing intimacy is what happens next.*

In most cases the wounds we receive from suffering and rejection are the places from which relationship ruptures grow and bloom. Even when we heal from those wounds, the scars and the memories are still there—and the pain can get easily reactivated by a stressful argument, a harsh retort, or even the most minor slight.

Ruptures within relationships are going to happen—we need to be okay with that truth. But what really matters is what we do afterward. Do we move away from, move against, or move toward the other person?

When we sin we rupture our relationship with God. And God shows us what to do afterward. He moves toward us. He moved toward his people in the garden ("Where are you?"); he moved toward his people after the flood (that promise tied with a rainbow); and he moved toward us under a star, in a manger, across a sea, and on the cross.

SOUND FAMILIAR?

Harvard researcher Shawn Achor once talked to a tax auditor who was very depressed. As they were talking about why, the auditor mentioned that one day during a break at work, he made an Excel spreadsheet listing all the mistakes his wife had made during the past six weeks. (I am not making this up.) (from *I'd Like You More*)

BIBLE CONNECT

Work through some of these questions with your group, but don't feel pressured to talk about them all. Finish any questions you don't get to in your individual time later in the week. If you are short on time, focus on questions 1, 4, 6, 7, and 9.

1. The story of Joseph shows us a young man who learned about empathy through suffering. Read Genesis 37:1-11. How did Joseph's brothers feel about him? How did Joseph feel about his brothers?

2. Joseph was betrayed by his brothers, sold into slavery, betrayed by his master's wife, and put in prison. Read Genesis 39:20-23. Who was with Joseph in his suffering? What effect did that have on Joseph?

3. Read Genesis 40:6, 7. How do these verses show a change in Joseph from the boy who told his dreams to his brothers?

4. Read Genesis 43:29-34; 45:1-7, 14, 15; 50:15-21. What can you learn from these verses about what effects suffering, rejection, and ruptured relationships had on these men?

5. Ortberg discusses the difference between grumbling and groaning as expressions of suffering. In our relationships with each other, groaning means raising our complaints with the person who is at the heart of our conflict. Grumbling means talking about that person to anyone else. In our relationships with God, groaning means lifting our laments about our suffering directly to God. Grumbling would be complaining about our disappointment with God to anyone else who would listen. Where can you find groaning and grumbling in Joseph's story? Why does groaning build intimacy while grumbling erodes intimacy?

6. Many generations after the time of Joseph, a boy-meets-girl story unfolds in the town of Sychar, near the land Jacob had given to Joseph. It's the story of Jesus meeting a Samaritan woman in the heat of the day. Read John 4:1-30, 39-42 and answer the following question: Jesus made a "bid" to connect with the woman. What was his bid, and how did she respond?

7. Think about these characteristics of the Samaritan woman:

   • She was poor. A woman of means would have had a servant do the work of hauling water.

   • She was trying to avoid society. People would generally go fetch the water during the cooler parts of the day, yet here she was at noon.

   • She had not only experienced societal rejection (from Jews and from her own town), she had experienced personal suffering through her broken relationships with men.

Look carefully at what Jesus said and did in this story.
What can we learn from the way he addressed her various
levels of suffering and rejection? Consider what another
rabbi might have done in his place (Samaritan women
were considered unclean by the Jews). What might that
interaction have looked like?

8. The Samaritan woman went from hiding and dodging in
   her shame to speaking out. Though we don't know what
   happened with her and her not-husband, what can we
   observe about how her relationships changed?

9. What do you see in the story of the Samaritan woman
   that reminds you of your own situation? What is different?
   How do you think you would have responded to Jesus'
   bid to connect?

GO OUT
- Pray together.
- Discuss where and when the next meeting will be.
- Exchange contact information as needed.
- Use the space below to jot down a couple thoughts
  you want to remember and revisit before your
  next meeting.

_____

_____

_____

_____

OUT OF GROUP

PRAY

As you go through this study, remember to stay in communication with God. If you are currently going through a period of suffering, ask God to sit with you in that suffering. Ask him to send someone to care for you through that suffering. If you are nursing the sting of rejection, talk to God about your feelings—groan to God about your disappointment, frustration, and shame. Honestly ask God to reveal to you ways that you have inflicted suffering on others or ways that you have rejected others. Ask forgiveness for times that you have grumbled about God or other people.

Slightly Awkward Exercise 1

Take on the role of a suffering detector. Pick a day when you know you will have to interact often with other people. As you go through your day remember to pay attention to every person you meet: the salesperson on the phone, your children, the dry cleaner clerk, the bus driver, the soccer coach, your spouse, etc. Listen to their responses to your question, "How are you doing today?" Don't just accept "Fine" as an answer and keep walking. Listen and ask a follow-up question such as "Really? You don't sound so fine—has something gone wrong today?" Or "Glad to hear it—what's been going well today?"

· · · · · · · · · ·

CONNECT AGAIN

Go back and think through the things you did and talked about with your group. Reflect on these things and write about your impressions.

What's something new you learned about the people in your group?

_____

_____

_____

_____

What's something you learned or revisited about yourself?

_____

_____

_____

_____

What have you learned in this session that will help you make deeper connections with people and increase intimacy? What have you learned about ways of eroding intimacy?

_____

_____

_____

_____

_____

_____

_____

_____

Make a list of groans for your week. What things are causing you to feel badly? Circle the ones that you've grumbled to others about. What could you do instead of grumbling?

_____

_____

_____

_____

_____

_____

_____

_____

Slightly Awkward Exercise 2

Practice some rejection therapy. In *I'd Like You More*, Ortberg tells the story of Jia Jiang, a man who had experienced various kinds of rejection. He didn't want his fear of rejection to keep him from taking risks, so he tried a behavioral treatment called "rejection therapy." The idea is that you make outrageous requests—ones you know will be rejected—so that you eventually get used to hearing the word no, and that word starts to lose its power. Two examples of what Jia Jiang asked for are a burger refill at a fast-food restaurant and a German Shepherd haircut at a PetSmart. What outrageous requests can you make? Try making ten outrageous requests this week. If you need help with ideas, ask some fellow group members. Take some selfies to document your exercises of rejection therapy and post those so your group can see them.

· · · · · · · · · ·

Write down all the sources of shame that you are currently carrying around with you. It could be shame about being abandoned by your father when you were a child. Or shame about losing a job. Or you could just feel ashamed of cheating on your diet. Or about bad feelings you keep having toward someone you work with. Over the top of every entry on your list write the words "no condemnation" (making the original entry virtually unreadable). Next to each entry on your list, write one positive thing you know about yourself.

_____

_____

_____

_____

_____

_____

_____

_____

_____

_____

Read through the Bible verses that you talked about with your group. Be sure also to read through any that you didn't have time to discuss in the group. What struck you about the story of Joseph?

_____

_____

_____

What stood out for you about the story of the Samaritan woman?

_____

_____

_____

_____

Read Romans 15:7. What kind of acceptance do you have in Christ today? What kind of acceptance do you need to offer to someone else?

_____

_____

_____

_____

Slightly Awkward Exercise 3

Perform a gratitude audit on one of your close relationships. Make a copy of the chart on the next page, or fill it in using pencil so that you can erase and use it again, if you wish. Write your person's name on the line at the top. Then fill out the rest of the chart, thinking of different qualities or facts or experiences of that person that you are grateful for. Then take a picture of that chart and send it to the person the chart is about. Try doing this every week and see what happens!

THINGS I AM GRATEFUL FOR ABOUT _____	
Something true.	
Something noble.	
Something right.	
Something pure.	
Something lovely.	
Something admirable.	
Something excellent.	
Something praiseworthy.	

Before your next session—as you interact with friends, roommates, your spouse, your kid, your parent, your boss, or anyone else close to you—consider John Ortberg's strategies for moving from rupture in relationships to repair. Consider even small ruptures, since small ones build up into bigger ones over time.

1) Stop. When you feel your emotions rising, take a break. Go for a walk. Go to the bathroom. Calm down.

2) Ask. When you've calmed yourself, ask these two questions: Why am I angry/frustrated/sad/feeling what I'm feeling? and What do I want?

3) Caution. Consider your approach carefully. Remember that how you begin a conversation can significantly affect how it will end.

4) Yield. Slow down enough to recognize what the other person is experiencing right now.

Try reminding yourself of these symbols as you interact with people this week. Jot some notes down here so you can remember what worked and what didn't.

_____

_____

_____

_____

_____

_____

_____

PRAY

Pray this prayer:

Man of Sorrows, you understand my suffering more than I do. You experienced the pain of being rejected by the world. Help me to strip away any masks that I use to hide my pain or shame. Help me to let go of my insecurity. Help me to be honest with those who are closest to me about the cause of my negative feelings. Help me to stop condemning myself. Enable me to separate my regret about what I've done from my confidence about who you've created me to be. Help me to rest in that confidence as I seek to repair and grow my relationships with the people I care about the most. Amen.

PREPARE

Do the following before your next group session:

- Read chapters 13 and 14 of *I'd Like You More* (if you have a copy).
- Continue to practice being a suffering detector whenever you can.
- Check your email/text/social media site to see if anyone has posted evidence of his or her rejection-therapy exercises.
- Find out if you need to bring any food item to your next group meeting.
- Think about this big question: Who will cry at my funeral?

REAL AND CLOSE

When I think about love, I think about a table.
But it's not healthy for us to sit at the table forever.

IN GROUP

BE PREPARED TO

eat together

talk

get real

serve

laugh

pray

OPEN UP

- Pray.
- Make and/or enjoy a meal or snacks together.
  (The host or leader of the group will provide
  instructions beforehand for what to bring.)

- Join an icebreaker activity led by the leader.
- Watch the optional video introduction.
- Discuss: Does sharing our best friends with others cause us to grow closer together or does it cause us to lose our best friends?

CONNECT

This is our last session! But thankfully, it isn't the end of our journey to closer relationships and deeper connections. Instead, this is just the beginning.

We're sure you've already started using some of the ideas in this study to reach out, to connect, to commit, to tear down, and to repair. And by now you can probably say *intimacy* without hesitating even slightly or mumbling it under your breath.

We started out this journey at the table. It was good to spend time there—listening together, learning about one another, laughing, and sharing in some good food for thought (and for the stomach). But it's time to push our chairs back and move on.

But where will we go first? And who will go with us?

In Chapter 13 of *I'd Like You More*, Ortberg discusses the idea of thinking about who will cry at your funeral. This isn't some kind of morbid game, but it's a way to focus on what really matters. And who really matters. It helps us prioritize the time we spend with people and the energy we put into our relationships.

Talk about it:

- In our intro activity, we talked about who would be at our funeral. But who will not be there?

Specifically, of the people we spend time thinking about, reading about, watching on TV, working with, bumping into, and so forth in any given year, which of those people are we really investing in? And which ones should we be investing less time and energy in? (For example, those people on Netflix I spent 8 hours of my life with last Saturday probably won't show up to my funeral.)

- Am I giving the best of my time and my life to the people who will miss me when I'm gone?
- How am I serving the people that I care about the most?

Easy Group Exercise: Speed Ritual Practice
Follow the leader's instructions to participate in this speedy version of daily rituals.

Think about it:
- What is my typical greeting to the people who are closest to me?
- How have I been showing appreciation to people I care about?
- When I'm gone for a week, does anyone really notice? When other people are gone, do I notice?

When Jesus was having his Last Supper with his friends, there came a point when—as sometimes happens between brothers and friends at the table—a quarrel broke out: Who was the greatest? Jesus answered the dispute with "Who is greater, the one who is at the table or the one who serves? Is it not the one who is at the table? But I am among you as one who serves" (Luke 22:27). He then told them he was conferring on them a kingdom, with the implication being that in this kingdom, they—like him—would serve.

And then Jesus said, "Wanna go for a walk?" (or something like that), and they went out to the Mount of Olives—for centuries the source of the oil used to anoint kings and high priests. And there this King of kings and our intimate high priest knelt on the ground and prayed so earnestly, sweat poured from his brow like drops of blood. And his friends were there with him in his suffering. And he was there . . . with all of us in *our* suffering.

Perhaps he thought, *Who will cry at my funeral?* And, *Will they remember I said I was coming back?*

> He loves the worst person in his world more than you love the best person in yours.

In some of his last words to his best friends, Jesus made himself clear. The way to get real—to get real about getting close, to get real about having deep, loving, eternity-shaped connections with people—is to serve one another.

Ortberg puts it this way: "The fellowship of the early church centered on the dinner table. They shared the Lord's supper there. It was a place of great intimacy. But the measure of the greatness of their community was not the experience of intimacy; it was the extent to which their intimacy with God and with one another overflowed to the blessing of those not yet at the table" (*I'd Like You More*).

It may not be your fault, but it certainly is your time.

There's a world out there that is hurting and suffering—alone in the dark. It's a world that's waiting for us to get up from the table. Waiting for us to go and make disciples, to tell them that Jesus is with us—always, and to the very end.

Talk about it:

- Ortberg refers to the act of having a relationship with those outside your circle of intimacy as "outimacy." He says, "Remember, *intimacy* without *outimacy* leads to stagnation and death. Once you have experienced true intimacy, it is your great commission to share it with others." What do you think about that? How is it good for a community to move outside that community?
- Is the level of happiness within a community always a good measure of success? Why or why not? How true do you think this statement is: "People who are deeply connected are deeply happy"?
- How could the church do a better job at being the church in the world?

Slightly Awkward Group Exercise: It's Our Time

Follow your leader's instructions to prepare for an act of service you can do together.

Think about it:

- How do you feel when you are serving others?
- What are some habits or practices in your church family that might make it easy to get caught up in just talking with and serving one another inside the church—instead of going out?
- Think about this statement: "When it comes to love . . . it turns out giving is the only path to receiving."

We can find many examples in the Bible of people who shared experiences with each other, developed a bond, and then went out and served others. Of course, the greatest example of this is Jesus. "If intimacy is shared experience, then the Incarnation is its greatest expression, its highest articulation, its deepest sacrifice" (Ortberg, *I'd Like You More*). Jesus not only wrote the last word on intimacy, he was the Word. And in his fleshy, messy, broken, and scarred self, he showed us what it looks like to live a fully committed life—a life so real, it hurts. And he showed us how to get real too.

♥ SOUND FAMILIAR?

In *I'd Like You More*, John Ortberg envisions where we can see love in the world: "It's in the marriage and parenting. It's in the family and friends. It's in the murmur of my parents' voices when

I'm a drowsy little boy in the back seat of the car and all is right with the world. It's in the joy of my friend Rick, who just became a grandfather, and tells me that having a grandchild slows you way down, because you have to adjust to Baby Time. And babies don't do hurry. . . . It's around the table in a little breakfast room on Brendenwood Terrace that time cannot erase from my mind."

BIBLE CONNECT

Work through some of these questions with your group, but don't feel pressured to talk about them all. Finish any questions you don't get to in your individual time later in the week. If you are short on time, focus on questions 1, 3, 6-9.

1. As we consider what it means to move away from the table and out to serve in the world, let's look at the life of a woman named Dorcas. We don't know a lot about Dorcas herself, but what we do know can be found in Acts 9—the same chapter in the Bible in which Paul's conversion experience is recorded, so Dorcas is in good company. Read Acts 9:36-43 and jot down or talk about all the facts you can gather about Dorcas—what was she known for, where did she live, who were her friends, what happened to her, etc.

2. What can you guess about Dorcas since you know how much she was able to do for others while she was alive, and how her body was treated after she died? Who cried for Dorcas?

3. Have three members of your group each read one of these
    sets of verses, all from Acts 9: a) verses 1a, 22, and 31;
    b) verses 32-35; c) verses 37, 40, and 42. Talk about the
    similarities and differences in these three stories of trans-
    formation. What did it take in each for change to occur?
    What was the effect?

4. Read Romans 12:1-5. What kind of sacrifice must you
    make to experience transformation? What kind of effect
    could your transformation have on the family of believers?
    How have you been affected by the transformation of
    others?

5. Read James 1:27. What is the religion that is considered
    pure? Why do you think James pairs the two ideas of
    serving others and not being polluted by the world? Read
    on in James 2:1-17. What in those verses might tell us
    what James considered as being "pollution"? What else do
    we learn about his thoughts on serving others?

6. For the rest of our study, we'll turn from thinking about
    how we can connect with and serve others to thinking
    about how we can connect with and serve Jesus. In
    Chapter 14 of I'd Like You More, John Ortberg refers to
    the Bible as a love story—a story of God's love for his
    people. And at the heart of that story lies the key to the
    mystery of intimacy. The story begins with God's searching
    in the garden ("Where are you?"), and it culminates in
    Jesus' great submission in the garden ("Not as I will, but
    as you will"), and the resurrection that came three days
    later. Though we in our humanness separated ourselves

from God, God became fully human to bring us back together—to share in our experience. Let's look at some of the human moments in Jesus' life, beginning with Luke 2. Read verses 1-7, 21-24, 42-48, and 51. Consider what aspects of the experiences in those verses are like any human's experience (share your own stories too), and what aspects are different from our own life experiences.

7. Let's continue considering Jesus' life experiences. Read these verses from the beginning of his ministry in Luke 4:1, 2, 16, 22-30 and in Luke 5:15, 16. What about these experiences stands out to you? What reminds you of experiences you have had?

8. Consider these emotional experiences of Jesus: when he was surprised—Luke 7:9; when he was moved—verses 12, 13; when he was annoyed by criticism—verses 33, 34; when he was fed up—9:41; when he was fired up—12:49-51; when he was snappy—13:31-33; when he was grieved—19:41-44; when he was in anguish—22:44. Can you relate to these experiences? What does it mean to you to know that Jesus had these emotions?

9. Consider these physical and social experiences of Jesus: when he was tired—John 4:6; when his mom embarrassed him—John 2:4; when he needed some time on his own—Matthew 14:13, 22, 23; when his mouth got him into hot water—John 8:58, 59 and John 10:31-33; when some of his fans left him—John 6:66; when he was betrayed by a friend—Matthew 26:47-50; when he was hurt and humiliated—Luke 22:63-65, John 18:22, 19:1-3; when

his body was taken and buried—Luke 23:53, John 19:38-42. What do you learn about Jesus from these experiences? What does it mean to you to know Jesus went through these things?

GO OUT

- Pray together.
- Talk about where you can meet together to perform your act of service.
- Discuss next steps (either your next study material, where people can go to learn and grow more as disciples, etc.).
- Use the space below to jot down a couple thoughts you want to remember.

_____

_____

_____

_____

OUT OF GROUP

PRAY

As you conclude this study, commit to staying in communication with God. Look back in your notes and remember any exercises you tried that worked for you (or ones you haven't tried yet). Put reminders in your phone or on your calendar to try those exercises again. It takes a while to adopt new good habits, or to change old bad ones. Use technology to your advantage. A simple alarm set to remind you to greet someone every day could be the thing that helps you stay on the path to developing deeper connections. Keep the conversation about your fears going between you and God. Keep bringing to Jesus your feelings about the people in your life and the experiences you've had with them. And continue to ask God to show you opportunities to get closer to others.

Slightly Awkward Exercise 1

Fill in this simple chart on the next page. Consider your regular weekly activities. Shade in the boxes that represent times when you feel most "with it"—when your mind is sharp, when you have energy, or when you are fully involved in what you are doing. Use the darkest shading for the times you feel at your best, lighter shading for times when you are not so engaged (or when you are tired, zoning out, etc.), and leave boxes completely blank when you are asleep or otherwise completely disengaged.

	SUN	MON	TUE	WED	THU	FRI	SAT
4-5am							
6-7							
7-8							
8-9							
9-10							
10-11							
11-12pm							
12-1							
1-2							
2-3							
3-4							
4-5							
5-6							
6-7							
7-8							
8-9							
9-10							
10-11							
11-12am							
12-1							
1-2							
2-3							
3-4							

When you have finished filling in the chart, look back over the way you've shaded it and consider this: In the darkest times, the times you are at your best—who is with you? Who is getting to share in the best of you? And in your lighter times, who is with you then? Who consistently gets to share in the times when you are least alert and engaged? At which times are you most likely to be communicating with God?

. . . .

CONNECT AGAIN

Go back and think through the things you did and talked about with your group. Reflect on these things and write about your impressions.

What's something new you learned about the people in your group?

_____

_____

_____

_____

_____

What's something you learned or revisited about yourself?

_____

_____

_____

_____

_____

What is one new thing you learned about intimacy or connecting with others during the time with your group?

_____

_____

_____

_____

Think about the idea that "*intimacy* without *outimacy* leads to stagnation and death." Do you agree or disagree with this statement? What does the idea of outimacy mean to you? What relationships do you have now that could benefit from some outimacy?

_____

_____

_____

_____

Slightly Awkward Exercise 2

At his last gathering around a table with his friends, before he was arrested, Jesus did something unusual. He washed their dirty feet (John 13:1-17). There are a couple of interesting things about this act. One is that Jesus could have served his friends in any way—he could have brought them food, he could have fetched water, he could have made them comfortable with pillows, he could have simply placed a basin of water out for them to wash themselves. He could have done many things, but he chose the lowliest thing. He chose the dirtiest chore, and the one considered perhaps most unlikely for a rabbi to perform—to be so intimately associated with a part of the body that is still considered vulgar in much of the world (particularly in some Asian and Middle Eastern cultures).

The second thing to note is that this exercise required audience participation—the disciples had to submit to being washed. Peter tried to refuse Jesus, in fact, but Jesus said that Peter would "have no part" with Jesus unless he allowed his feet to be washed. The men had to let their Lord see the dirt on them and wipe it away.

For this exercise, seek to do the lowliest thing. Do the least thing you can do for someone else. And let someone else do the least for you. What is the one chore at your workplace that no one wants to do? Do that. What is the one thing in your house that everyone wants to pass off onto someone else? Do that. Change the diapers, pick up the dog poo, clean the toilet, take out the trash. Do the least thing. Then let someone help you with your lowliest task. And remember, sometimes those lowly things don't involve any kind of dirt you can see—more often than not, the nitty-gritty stuff of life comes in the form of emotional and social interactions. Drive someone to get a dreaded test done, go with a friend to an AA meeting, encourage a student before a final exam, be willing to accompany a person to her high school reunion.

Ask these questions of the people in your life: "What's the hardest thing you have on your plate this week? What's the thing you are most often dreading?" When you've got answers, figure out how to help them with those things.

Then ask yourself the same questions. When you've got answers, reach out and ask some people to help you with your lowly things. Don't fret about the dirt they might see—let them see the dirt of your life and help to wipe it away.

· · · · · · · · · ·

.What about serving others is easy for you? What about serving others is hard? What experiences have you had with serving others as part of a group?

_____

_____

_____

_____

Read through the Bible verses that you talked about with your group. Be sure also to read through any that you didn't have time to discuss in the group. What did you think about the stories of transformation from Acts 9? Have you ever been personally affected by someone's service or generosity? How did being on the receiving end of that change you?

_____

_____

_____

_____

Consider the experiences of Jesus that were discussed in the Bible study questions. Think of one experience Jesus had that you can easily relate to. Why do you relate to that experience so well?

_____

_____

_____

_____

Complete this sentence: When I think about how Jesus _____
_____, I feel closer to him.

_____

_____

_____

_____

Consider one experience Jesus had while he was living on this earth
that you find difficult to understand. What makes it so hard for you
to relate to that experience?

_____

_____

_____

_____

Complete this sentence: I'd like to understand more about how Jesus

_____

_____

_____

_____

Ortberg began talking about our relationship with God by looking
at the story of God and the first humans. He said God came to walk
in the garden and put out the "simplest bid for intimate connection,
repeated by every human being who ever lived: 'Want to go for a
walk?'" The man and woman then did not want to—or maybe they
did, but felt they were too ashamed to say so. What about you? Do
you want to go for a walk? Do you want to go for a walk with God?

What would you like to say to him? What subjects would you be hoping he might cover? Imagine how that conversation might go and write it out here.

_____

_____

_____

_____

Slightly Awkward Exercise 3

The subtitle of Ortberg's book—the book this study has been based on—is *Getting Real about Getting Close*. But it could have also been *Getting Closer to Being Real*. In the last chapter of the book, Ortberg talks about what real intimacy looks like, and how Jesus lived that out as an example for us. Ortberg gives some specific examples of ways he would like to be more real:

- To own my own story
- To understand my own worth
- To let go of other's opinions of me
- To be healed of everything that makes me want to hide: greed, lust, judging, deceit, pettiness, envy
- To be genuine—so that what you see is what you get

What would you add to this list? Write below your own wish list for being real:

_____

_____

_____

_____

Think of one step you can take this week toward being more real with God, and more real with others. Practice taking that step every day and push yourself to do more.

· · · · · · · · · ·

Before you leave this study, go back to the first session and find the intimacy quotient surveys you took about your intimacy levels with others and with God. Go through those statements and questions again and see if any of your answers have changed. If they haven't, spend some time thinking about why that is, and what you need to do to improve your connections with others. What do you need to do to get closer to God?

PRAY

Pray this prayer based on 1 John 4:10:

God, I am drawn to love you because you are so good. And when you do good things for me, I feel that love even more. But I want to love like you do. To love others not for what they can do, but to love no matter what—in good times and bad, in the times when things are easy and free and in the times when things are messy and tangled. I want to share in the experiences of others in a way that creates connection. I want to know Jesus better, so I can see what real human life looks like, and follow his example. I want to be real—with you, with my loved ones, with anyone. Thank you for sending your Son to us; for letting him sacrifice his perfect, pure, unburdened life to take on our messy, hard, and tangled days. Thank you for his love that makes us able to become real, for always. Amen.

GET REAL

As you leave this study

- Think of someone who might like to share your copy of *I'd Like You More*. If you don't have a copy yet, consider getting one and reading it.
- Be aware of how you are spending your time this week and who you are spending it with.
- Consider ways you can do one of the "lowly things" for someone in the coming weeks.
- If you won't be meeting with this particular group anymore, talk with your fellow group members to see how you can stay connected. If you will be continuing to meet together, discuss what will be the next subject you will focus on.
- Think about this big statement: "Intimacy with God isn't mostly something I *do*, but something I receive."

Notes

Notes

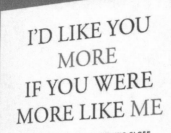

 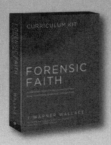  

Journey with Your Church through the Bible's 40 Biggest Ideas

Are you looking to increase Bible engagement at your church? This 8-week church-wide program opens up the whole Bible to those who read Scripture regularly, as well as those who are just beginning. *The Good Book Church Campaign Kit* explores 40 key Bible chapters that lay the foundation for understanding the entirety of Scripture. As your church learns more about the Bible's biggest ideas, you will be prepared to step out into the world to offer joy, peace, and hope to your community.

Deron Spoo is the pastor of First Baptist Church in Tulsa, Oklahoma. Over the past 16 years, Spoo has guided the church as it transitions from being simply a downtown church to a regional church committed to urban ministry. His television devotionals, *First Things First*, reach 100,000 people each week. Spoo is a graduate of Southwestern Baptist Theological Seminary. He and his wife, Paula, have three children.

Available in print and digital
wherever books are sold